Essential Jobs

We Need Manufacturing Workers

by Brienna Rossiter

FOCUS READERS
PIONEER

www.focusreaders.com

Focus Readers is distributed by North Star Editions:
sales@northstareditions.com | 888-417-0195

Produced for Focus Readers by Red Line Editorial.

Photographs ©: Shutterstock Images, cover, 1, 4, 6 (top), 6 (bottom), 8, 11, 12, 15, 18, 21; iStockphoto, 17

Library of Congress Cataloging-in-Publication Data
Library of Congress Cataloging-in-Publication Data is available on the Library of Congress website.

ISBN
978-1-63739-033-7 (hardcover)
978-1-63739-087-0 (paperback)
978-1-63739-194-5 (ebook pdf)
978-1-63739-141-9 (hosted ebook)

Printed in the United States of America
Mankato, MN
012022

About the Author

Brienna Rossiter is a writer and editor who lives in Minnesota.

Table of Contents

Chapter 1

Manufacturing

People use many items each day. They wear clothes. They play with toys. They use computers and phones. Factories **manufacture** all of these items.

There are many types of factories. Some of them make food. Others make **fuel** for airplanes or cars. Still others make **electronics**.

Workers help run all of these factories. They also package items and send them to stores.

Chapter 2

Making Materials

Many factories make **materials**. For example, some factories make paper. Some cut wood into boards. Some melt or mix metals. Others make cloth or plastic.

Factories use machines to do these jobs. Some workers **operate** machines. Others send the materials out. They load trucks or trains. The materials go to other factories or stores. There, people can use the materials to make **products**.

РАБОЧАЯ ИНСТРУКЦИЯ
A17a
PHILIPS
40PFT4100/60

Chapter 3

Making Products

Factories also put products together. Some make small parts. Others join many parts together. They make finished items. For example, some factories build cars.

Many factories use assembly lines. Items move on a belt or chain. One part is added at a time. Some workers add parts. Others check finished items. Workers sort and pack items, too.

Fun Fact

Factories use machines to do many jobs. But people still do some steps by hand.

Engineers

Engineers plan how factories work. They look at what job a factory will do. They split this job into steps. Engineers plan each step. Workers do some steps. Machines do others. They must all work together. Engineers use computers to test their plans. They try to make each step quick and easy.

Chapter 4

Safety

Many workers help factories run safely. Some workers **inspect** machines. They check for problems. Workers also fix broken parts.

Many factories create waste. Workers may help store waste. Or they may get rid of it. Workers find safe ways to do this. They try not to harm the **environment**.

Fun Fact

Factories can be dangerous. So, workers may wear helmets or gloves.

FOCUS ON

Manufacturing Workers

Write your answers on a separate piece of paper.

1. Write a sentence describing one thing workers do to help make factories safe.
2. If you owned a factory, what would you want it to make? Why?
3. What does an assembly line do?
   - A. store waste
   - B. pay workers
   - C. make items
4. Why would some factories make small parts?
   - A. Factories can't make large items.
   - B. Other factories can use these parts to build larger items.
   - C. Other factories can throw these parts away.

Answer key on page 24.

Glossary

electronics
Machines that use electricity to work.

environment
The natural surroundings of living things.

fuel
Material that is burned to create heat or power.

inspect
To check something carefully.

manufacture
To make things that will be bought or sold.

materials
The matter, such as cloth or metal, that a thing can be made from.

operate
To use or control a machine.

products
Items that are for sale.

To Learn More

BOOKS

Hansen, Grace. *How Is Peanut Butter Made?* Minneapolis: Abdo Publishing, 2018.

Tortland, Christy. *Heavy-Machine Operators on the Job.* Mankato, MN: The Child's World, 2020.

NOTE TO EDUCATORS

Visit **www.focusreaders.com** to find lesson plans, activities, links, and other resources related to this title.

Index

Answer Key: 1. Answers will vary; **2.** Answers will vary; **3.** C; **4.** B